SPEAKERS RESOURCE ORGANIZATION

Businesses Rely on Us...Audiences Remember Us!

Presents

How to
Conquer Conflict:

Business and Personal

Featuring:

Susan Bulfinch

Allan Himmelstein

Valerie Harper

ISBN-13: 978-1496016560

ISBN-10: 1496016564

Published 2014

Created and Designed by …
Be The Dream LLC

Publisher@BeTheDream.com

SPEAKERS RESOURCE ORGANIZATION

Want to spice up your next meeting?

Use a professional guest speaker from SRO.

The members of Speakers Resource Organization are seasoned professionals with a massive variety of industry backgrounds and expertise. They pride themselves in thought-provoking presentations and takeaways that land on your up-front-and-center bookshelf rather than a dark corner or round file.

Their clients -- corporations, non-profit groups, and business advisory groups -- repeatedly hire them for gold-standard facilitation and learning that sticks.

SRO delivers integrity with quality that exceeds client expectations. SRO is the vendor of choice for creating great events through information, sharing, and teaching.

Looking for a specific topic or timeframe? Let SRO assist you with either -- made-to-order for your event.

Contact info: info@speakersresourceorganization.com or any of the speakers presenting at today's event.

Table of Contents

Got Conflict? 1

How to Discuss Difficult Issues................... 11

Conquer Conflict in Your Life 17

Our Next Taster... 25

Meet Our Presenters 27

Bruce Benefiel 29

Susan Bulfinch.............................. 31

Dr. Richard Deems.................... 33

Jack Dermody........................ 35

Valerie Harper 37

Mary Henry 39

Allan Himmelstein 41

Karen Laughlin................................ 43

Dr. Kristine Quade 45

Ray Silverstein 47

Dr. Terri Trent.................................. 49

Elena Zee................................... 51

Got Conflict?

5 Styles for Responding to Conflict

SusanBulfinch@mediate.com

Phone: 480 209 1295

Fax: 480-209-1296

What is Conflict?

- a state of being incompatible, having an unresolved difference of opinion resulting in a disagreement and/or disharmony
- when two or more parties have an unresolved discrepancy in ideas or actions that result in a clash or struggle.

Conflict can be USEFUL AND POSITIVE when it brings problems into the open and motivates people to understand each other's perspective, encourages new ideas to bring about innovation and change. It can be DESTRUCTIVE when it causes negative emotions and stress, reduces necessary communication and emphasizes group differences and loyalty

What is the Cost of Conflict in the Workplace?

1. Wasted time
2. Reduced decision quality – information withheld or late
3. Turnover – HR expense
4. Restructuring – accommodating individuals in conflict
5. Sabotage / theft / damage
6. Lowered job motivation and satisfaction
7. Lost work time, absenteeism – reduced performance and productivity
8. Health costs
9. Loss of skilled employees

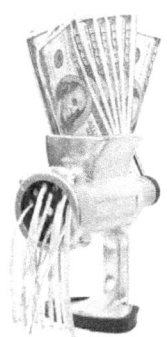

Strategies for Responding to Conflict

Most people are comfortable using one or two styles (strategies) for responding to conflict. However, no one strategy is effective in every situation. You'll be more successful in dealing with conflict when you learn to master all five strategies, enhance your ability to assess which style is most useful in each conflict situation, and consciously choose the best response.

AVOID OR WITHDRAW:
LOW ASSERTIVENESS AND LOW COOPERATION

You withdraw from the conflict situation, and do not immediately pursue either your concerns or those of another person. The outcome is not important to you. You might diplomatically sidestep the issue, postpone it until a better time, or withdraw from the situation. The conflict remains unresolved and neither of you wins.

What are benefits and drawbacks of this style?
Takes no time at all.   Nothing gets settled.

DIRECT OR COMPETE:
HIGH ASSERTIVENESS AND LOW COOPERATION

You pursue your own concerns at the other person's expense using whatever power is available to win. You may be standing up for your rights, defending a position because you believe you're right, or simply trying to win. People who use the competing style a lot are usually task-oriented and want to control the outcome. They are often highly productive and concerned with getting the job done.

What are benefits and drawbacks of this style?
Doesn't require a lot of time.   Promotes head butting.

ACCOMMODATE OR HARMONIZE:
LOW ASSERTIVENESS AND HIGH COOPERATION

You sacrifice your own concerns to the concerns of others. You want to keep the peace even though you disagree or would rather not do something. You may believe you're being generous or charitable when you obey someone else's wishes when they're against your own preferences. Opposite of Direct/Compete.

What are benefits and drawbacks of this style?

Others will like you; you're nice. You have little to no influence.

COMPROMISE OR SHARE:
MODERATE ASSERTIVENESS & MODERATE COOPERATION

You look for an expedient solution that *partially* satisfies both people. You give up more than if you choose to be Direct, but less than if you choose to Accommodate. You think this is a democratic way to resolve issues, but everyone is a bit unhappy about giving up something. It addresses an issue more directly than Avoiding, but not in as much depth as Collaborating.

What are benefits and drawbacks of this style?

Less time than collaborating. Nobody gets what they want.

COLLABORATE OR COOPERATE: HIGH ASSERTIVENESS AND HIGH COOPERATION

You assert your views while inviting others to share theirs. You welcome differences and work with others to find a creative solution that fully satisfies everyone's concerns. Takes time to explore issues and to discuss solutions.

What are benefits and drawbacks of this style?

Fully satisfies everyone's concerns. Takes a lot of time, energy.

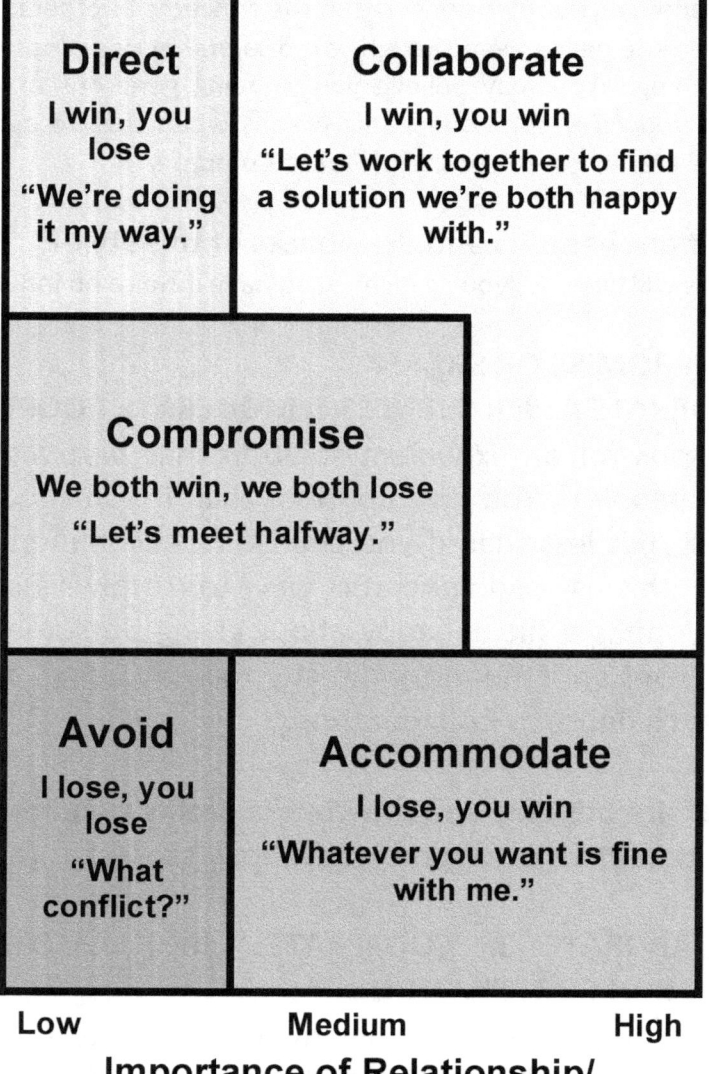

Strategically Choose Your Response

This assessment tool is designed to help you determine the optimal conflict resolution style to adopt in a given situation. Its underlying premise is that different conflict resolution strategies are indicated in different situations. Apply this tool to a real-life conflict, past, present, or future, to see how it works.

Situation Assessment Statements

Below are 10 pairs of statements. Each pair describes a conflict situation. Circle the letter of *the one statement from each pair* that you think fits your particular conflict situation best.

Even if neither statement fits your situation exactly, *you must choose one statement over the other*. Weigh the statements as accurately and honestly as possible.

Situation Assessment Statements	
P	I don't really care what the other party thinks of me after the conflict is over.
R	It is important that I have a good relationship with the other party once the conflict is over.
M	It won't be the end of the world if I don't resolve this conflict.
O	I have vital interests at stake in resolving this conflict.
P	I don't have a significant personal or business relationship with the other party.
R	My relationship with the other party is important for business or personal reasons.
M	The time and trouble needed to resolve this conflict may not be worth it in this case.

O	I expect the resolution of this conflict to be worth my while if it goes reasonably well.
P	In my relationship with the other party, there is very little sharing of feelings and information.
R	My relationship with the other party is based on shared feelings and information.
M	I don't expect resolving this conflict to affect future dealings with the other party.
O	I won't be surprised if resolving this conflict sets the pattern for many future conflicts.
P	My communication with the other party has been quite limited.
R	My communication with other party has been extensive.
M	I will not feel any worse about myself if I end up thinking I lost the conflict.
O	I won't feel really good unless I do well in this conflict.
P	I am not dependent upon the other party.
R	We have common interests because of the ways in which we are thrown together.
M	The issues at stake here are clear and straightforward.
O	I suspect there are important hidden factors at stake in this conflict.

Please count your letter scores and fill in the blanks below:

How many Ps did you circle?   _____

How many Rs did you circle?   _____

How many Os did you circle?   _____

How many Ms did you circle?   _____

Plot your scores to determine the conflict strategy that best matches your situation.

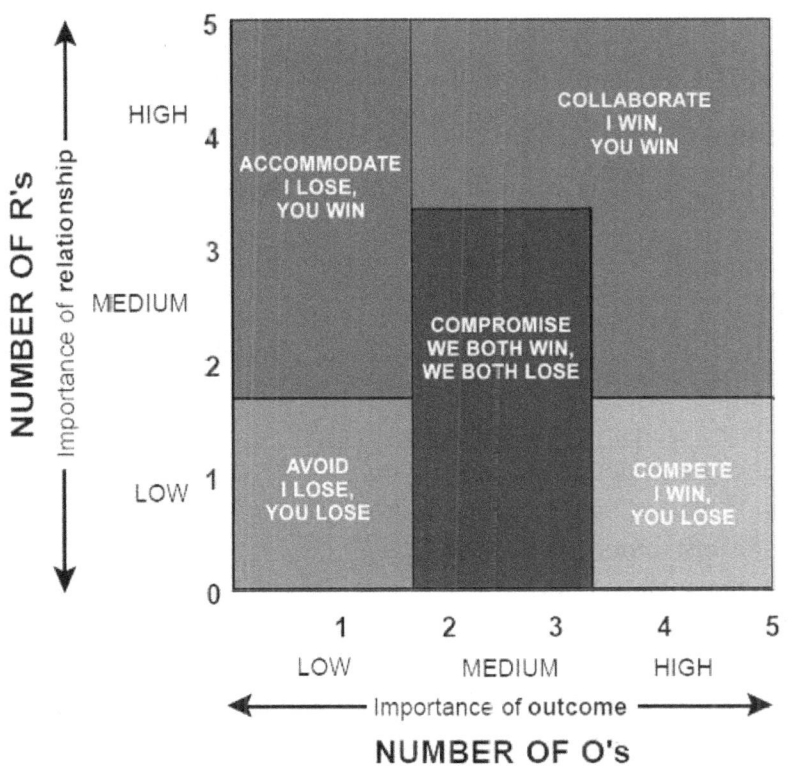

Remember no one strategy is effective in every situation. You will be more successful in dealing with conflict when you:

- Assess what is needed in each situation
- Skillfully and flexibly use all 5 strategies
- Consciously choose the most effective response

Sometimes you'll think it's more important to nurture the relationship. Sometimes you'll think it's more important to get what you want, and that the outcome is more important than the relationship. Sometimes you'll have to sacrifice one or the other. Sometimes you'll want to preserve the relationship and the outcome.

Use this strategy	With a situation:
Avoid	• in which neither outcome nor relationship matter to you.
Collaborate	• in which outcome and relationship are both very important.
Compete	• in which outcome is important but relationship is not.
Accommodate	• in which outcome is not important but relationship is.
Compromise	• in which outcome and relationship are both somewhat important to you.

Source: Hiam, Alexander, *Dealing with Conflict Instrument*, HRD Press

See also, related websites and resources such as:
http://www.kilmanndiagnostics.com/blog
http://www.kilmanndiagnostics.com/catalog/thomas-kilmann-conflict-mode-instrument
http://www.bus.iastate.edu/amt/Readings/Negotiation/Thomas%20Kilman.pdf
Cloke, Kenneth and Goldsmith, Joan: *Resolving Conflicts at Work.* 2000.
Stone, Douglas, Bruce Patton, Sheila Heen and Roger Fisher: *Difficult Conversations: How to Discuss What Matters Most.* 2000.

Notes:

How to Discuss Difficult Issues
with clients, bosses, and co-workers

Allan Himmelstein
Allan @SalesCoachAZ.com
480-656-3565

Sources of a dysfunctional organization

Inherent in many organizations is a dysfunctional working relationship between the sales force and accounting, production, research & development, and customer service. The source may be a client, a demanding sales person, and/or a business culture that lend itself to input. Frequently these companies do not have a clear culture, goals, or visions that they have articulated. This conflict is a de-motivator for the entire organization and results in costly turnover, and revenue and profit losses.

Never be afraid to "fire" a client that is abusive to your people, and consequently adversely affects the motivation of your team, turnover, and uncovered revenue and profit loss. With this being said, one must have the difficult conversations with clients before the "firing". The reason this conversation is so difficult is the fear of loss.

Some problems arising in a dysfunctional organization may be inherent in the behavior characteristics necessary to do different job functions:

a. Sales – Pro-active, ambivert*, juggle a lot of balls at once and lack of attention to details with a high sense of urgency.
b. Accounting – Be exact, detail oriented, and numbers oriented. Not totally time sensitive.
c. Production and Purchasing – Planning forward, follow procedures, process orientation. Strong time orientation.
d. Technical – Needs specific information to create new products. Sometimes more creative than exact.

*Ambivert is a personality trait including the qualities of both introversion and extroversion

Aside from general behavior characteristics, when people do not function as a team it truly affects the company's bottom line. Ask yourself the following questions:

1. Is your company experiencing high turnover either with your sales force or with internal staff?
2. Does everyone in your organization understand what each other needs and the time needed in order to do their job effectively?
3. Is there a written process that is adhered to when a new project or order comes to the company?
4. Do your sales people have a written process to give to the internal staff?
5. Does the internal staff feel that orders and projects are dumped in their laps without the necessary information to proceed?

If any or all of these points are happening in your company, then you are losing untold growth potential, revenues, and profits. Get the CFO, controller to do a true cost of sales to determine what the cost of turnover, rush orders, and poor quality *really* cost.

According to Patrick Lencioni* who wrote "The Five Dysfunctions of a Team" this is the list of areas to consider:

- Absence of Trust
- Fear of Conflict
- Lack of Communication
- Avoidance of Accountability
- Inattention to Results

*Patrick M. Lencioni, The Five Dysfunctions of a Team: A Leadership Fable, Jossey-Bass, 2002.

What can be done to alleviate the situation?

Communication is critical.

Below are some steps you can take to improve performance and productivity.

1. Leadership must really set forth what the corporate vision and values are without exception. Build a culture of corporate excellence.
2. Every department should define their particular process with the time line needed. This should be shared in writing and reviewed on a continual basis.
3. Emphasize the importance of having conflict and confrontation in a professional way. Attacking the arguments and not the person.
4. Utilize a systematic way of communication. Utilizing a CRM properly is a great way of developing a clear communication line.
5. Emphasize to everyone that no matter what their position is they are part of the sales process. Encourage sales to bring internal staff whether it is a CFO, production manager, or customer service person on sales calls.
6. Require your salespeople to spend a day working for the different departments to give them a deeper understanding of what they need to be effective.
7. Have regular team meetings to discuss the progress and have open suggestions to move forward. Make sure that there are specific actions with time lines.

Defining the Difficult Conversation

The Opportunity, Issue, or Threat	
What is the best Result that can be expected?	
What is the Worst thing that could happen?	
With Bullet Points define exactly what were the steps that led to this critical stage.	
What Action Has Already Been Taken?	
What will you need to attack the argument and NOT the person?	

Notes:

Conquer Conflict in Your Life

Valerie Harper
balancewealth@gmail.com
480-415-8075

Conflict is a state of opposition in actions, ideas, interests, or personalities. Struggles can result from incompatible or opposing needs, drives, wishes or demands.

> Words that describe conflict: opposition, warfare, antagonism, disagreement, dispute, controversy, discord, disturbance, interference.

What are some words that come to your mind when you think of conflict?

> Understanding conflict allows us to achieve resolution, have our needs met and understand the other person better, so we can maintain or restore connection and harmony.

What is conflict?

> Conflict can be an opportunity for growth. It is an opportunity to get to know the truth of someone or something. Understanding what conflict is and what causes it can help us more effectively reach resolution.

Why does it occur?

Full blown conflicts occur because communication has broken down. It can also be caused by selfish concern for one's own interests, without seeking to simultaneously meet the other person's needs.

Where does it come from?

Dueling wants, needs, ideas and poor or ineffective communication styles.

How might we respond to get the most out of any conflict whether it is internally or externally driven?

Learn to quiet the complaints of the mind enough to hear what the real complaint is.

How are conflicts affecting your life?

Many difficulties arise from conflict. The inability to resolve conflict causes forms of poverty in:

Love, Marriage, Health, Career, Money, Children & Family, Business Connections, Peace

What do we do about conflict?

1) We have to recognize it. We all have a different threshold for conflict that either sensitizes or desensitizes our ability to detect it. Our conditioning determines how we respond.
2) Understand your positioning within the conflict. What are you responsible for and what are you not responsible for?
3) Position yourself in the best way for resolution. (Always do this by making it your goal to understand the other person's point of view.)
4) Develop skills for how to handle conflict before you find yourself in conflict. These skills will help you de-escalate conflict or confront it head on before the issue becomes a big problem.

When developing a better conditioning for response remember these key things

1) Identify the needs. (There are 8 types of needs.)
2) Communicate the needs effectively and clearly.
3) Eliminate negative and defensive responses by recognizing your different emotional states.

People are always acting out their psychologies. You can tell what people fear by what they are against. We can always take these strong emotions as an indication of a deep fear. The four main fears are:

1) Losing control
2) Losing value
3) Exclusion
4) Inefficacy

Resolving conflict in some cases begins with resolving the conflict within yourself first. When you are at peace, you bring that peace to the relationship. When you are in turmoil, it becomes more difficult to maintain the quality of connections in your relationships. In personal relationships, realizing that something has broken the connection may be necessary before resolution can begin. Do your best to resolve inner conflicts first.

10 Questions to Ask Yourself to Better Understand Your Internal Feelings Surrounding Your Conflict

1. What feels uncomfortable to you about what you are feeling?

2. What is the trigger of your anger and what are you really angry about underneath the emotional responses you are feeling?

3. How would you describe the negativity you feel toward someone else or the situation you are dealing with?

4. What unrealistic demands or obligations to you feel this situation is placing on you?

5. What needs of yours are being valued or devalued from others and how have you effectively communicated them? What unspoken words might actually be contributing to the conflict?

6. How might you more effectively communicate your needs in this situation without getting angry or blaming the other person?

7. In what ways have you asked for what you wanted but still didn't get what you needed? How might you begin to get what you want even though others may not be hearing you?

8. Is this person being realistic or unrealistic and how does this make you want to respond? What might be a better way of responding that would be more effective in helping you get what you want?

9. If you were to receive what you wanted what would that be?

10. How might you put yourself in a better position of power as you see this conflict through to its solution?

10 Steps to Minimizing the Damaging Effects of Conflict

1. Take a stand when someone is being mistreated. We thrive when we are amongst supportive groups. If you find someone let a coyote in the hen house so to speak, make a consorted group effort to eliminate, exclude or rid yourself of that person if they are unwilling to be kind to others. Be honest an upfront about why they are not a good fit. Remain neutral and matter of fact. Do not overemphasize care because they will play on your emotions. People who easily mistreat other people are manipulators. They don't care about you. Showing them a firm boundary that this behavior will not be tolerated is better than reinforcing bad behavior by playing into their emotions with insincere niceties. If they are a sociopath which means they might seek revenge, call in the support of other's. There is power in numbers.

2. Recognize bullying occurs in all stages, races and social classes in life. Bullying happens in the most subtle of forms. Do your best to recognize it. When you see it taking place, validate another person's experience by stating the facts of what you see occurring. Then offer support. Remember, bullies are usually master manipulators. The last thing they want to usually do is to tell the truth. Refrain from the need to prove or convince them of anything. This can be how they distract you enough to begin taking from you.

3. When good hearted people start responding in passive aggressive ways it is usually because they have a hard time articulating their needs. They instead project the problem onto the other person. As an effective communicator, you may want to ask them straight out what they need. This might help the articulate what is happening to eliminate the passive aggressive behavior and resolve conflict quickly. If you are engaging with someone who has a mood disorder they may need to cycle out of their emotional process alone and the best thing is to not take things personally.

4. Take time to nurture the people around you while remembering you are responsible for yourself. Do your best to tend to your needs and care for other people's needs when you can. Take care of yourself first while considering others too. Make sure your caring ways come in the form of consideration and not caretaking which has more of a co-dependent nature.

5. When your emotional reserves are low do your best to contain your own conflict. Even if you are not causing harm to another person, excessively talking about your problems can cause conflict in the air. Find things that are uplifting and inspiring to talk about. Do your best to contain conflicts so they don't get the best of you. When you do need to talk about a problem, find someone you can trust that can actually support you by giving you a solid perspective.

6. In your heart, always remain positive. In your thinking remain realistic. Magical thinking around conflict tends to backfire. The truth is the majority of people are not that skilled at resolving conflicts without going to battle. Be mindful of how you are positioning yourself within a conflict and do your best to extract the opportunity that arises from any challenge. Always seek the fastest route to harmony while standing your ground.

7. As you move through life there are possibilities for inner and outer conflicts daily. Don't assume the truth of anything until you have a chance to sit emotionless with it. Observing the real problem. Be very mindful of the movements you make in the form of actions or words spoken. Keep a neutral demeanor and take nothing personal. A defensive response could detonate another person's emotional landmine. Remain true to who you are and do your best to work your way out of the chaotic condition by keeping your word and maintaining focus on resolution.

8. Where your attention goes, energy flows. Detach from all the superfluous details of the complaint and return to a state of peace, wellness and homeostasis by letting the whole thing go in your mind. It is easier to feel resolve when the other person's defenses are no longer attacking. However, you can find peace at any moment by returning to an inner state of mental and emotional balance simply by remaining neutral; refusing to fight; not taking any of it personally and taking actions that you know are the best to lead you back to happiness and joy.

9. When the conflicts get piled so high in your life, recognize the organizational challenge to manage your energy while effectively moving back into a state of peace. What problems are not yours to solve? Which ones can you let go of knowing they are not your own? What fears might you face that would help you grow into a stronger person? Allow the natural process of life to transition you into your next experience.

10. The best way to eliminate stress around conflict is to get very comfortable with it. Make peace with conflict and you make peace with life.

Valerie Harper is the creator of True Wealth Consulting. She assists people in discovering their inner wealth for outer success. She offers a unique approach to resolving the inner conflicts that help resolve financial issues, relationship problems and health imbalances. For more information on what her consultations entail, log onto www.valharper.com or contact her directly at 480-415-8075.

Our Next Taster...

How to Navigate Through Communication Missteps

Have you ever ended a personal or business relationship because of a misunderstanding? Have you ever been on the verge of closing a deal and then the clients change their mind and you don't have a clue why? Have you had conversations that seemed to go nowhere and you wanted to ask a personal or business partner, "*Do you understand the words that are coming out of my mouth*?!"

This workshop is designed to shed light on understanding how to gain insight into how people listen to what you say and to also navigate through a communication misstep in your professional career. You will learn:

- How to turn a career blunder into a valuable learning lesson and to prevent a reoccurrence
- Define contingencies and procedures to mitigate risk to your professional brand
- Actions to rebuild relationships with impacted peers, management and/or clients
- Seven ineffective ways people listen and how they impact communication
- How to recognize ineffective listening and techniques to resolve potential backlash

Wednesday, May 7th
9:00 AM – 10:30 AM

Check our website for more details, location and to register
www.SpeakersResourceOrganization.com

Meet Our Presenters

Bruce Benefiel 29

Susan Bulfinch 31

Dr. Richard Deems 33

Jack Dermody 35

Valerie Harper 37

Mary Henry 39

Allan Himmelstein 41

Karen Laughlin... 43

Dr. Kristine Quade 45

Ray Silverstein 47

Dr. Terri Trent.. 49

Elena Zee.... 51

SPEAKERS RESOURCE ORGANIZATION

Bruce 'Zen' Benefiel

 Bruce 'Zen' Benefiel, Founder/Owner and Chief Possibilities Coagulator at Be The Dream, LLC, is an author, speaker on holistic systems, project planning and self-development. He was blessed with the ability to say yes, take risks and garner worlds of experience and success across several industries. His forte: putting people, places and things together to do amazing stuff. He's also helped many authors become self-published through his expertise in journalism and self-publishing.

A highly qualified educator and facilitator, his presentations are engaging, intelligent, timely and witty. His passion is personal development and self-awareness that leads to making sense common – the foundation for any endeavor or project. His expertise also includes facilitating 'partnering' workshops for large concerns – building, road and bridge construction to name a few – under the Team Partnering LLC banner. Want a quick paradigm shift? Ask him how 'Zen' happened.

Hot Topics:

The Shift: Challenge to Change: *Removing Liabilities, Limitations and Excuses*

- Brilliant Behaviors that Work to Increase Performance
- Relation-ships on the Ocean of Emotion and How To Sail Them
- Three Elements that Connect Everyone to All Things Productive
- Best Practices for Connecting & Follow Up Exercises to Stay Fit

Growing Your Dream w/ Social Media - *Mania to Metanoia*

- Metanoia – A Change of Mind that Gets Results
- Definition of Social Media & Resources, Strategies and Tactics
- What Social Media Can Do For You and HOW TO Do It
- Pitfalls of Poor Media and Relationship Management

29

Communication and Problem-Solving - Keys to Partnering

- Practicing the Principles of Partnering – Commitment, Communication, Integrity and Trust
- Creating a Charter/Mission with Goals and Objectives that are Measurable
- Teamwork and Responsibility in the Process of Issue Resolution
- Tools for Effective Communication that Empowers Excellence

New Millennial Business Management Models - *Making Sense Common*

- What is a New Millennial Mindset and Why Would I Want One?
- Holistic Systems Approach to Understanding Flow and Productivity
- Transparency without Travesty – Doing the Right Things Right
- Aspirations for Excellence to Creating an Action Plan that Achieves

10 Steps to Growing Your Business in Good or Bad Times - *An Holistic Approach*

- Sales and Customer Statistical Awareness – What's Your Number?
- Enhancing the Customer Experience – Customer-Centric Tactics
- Use of Technology Beyond the Distractions and Interruptions
- Creating a Culture & Community that Thrives in Today's Market

Susan Bulfinch

Susan Bulfinch, with over 25 years' experience in mediation and conflict resolution, is a professional *neutral* in private practice mediating family, employment, sexual harassment, commercial, small business, and real estate matters.

Susan mediates for the United States Postal Service REDRESS Program, Maricopa County Justice Courts and the Employment Mediation Panel for the American Arbitration Association. As an educator, Susan has lectured extensively on alternative dispute resolution and teaches two courses each spring at the University of California, Santa Barbara.

A graduate of Hampshire College and Southwestern University School of Law, Susan is past president of the Southern California Mediation Association, Arizona Association for Conflict Resolution, Maricopa County Association of Family Mediators and Metropolitan Business and Professional Women.

Hot Topics:

Mediation Skills for the Workplace

- Introduction of the mediation process and how it is used in the workplace
- Practice active listening and other communication tools
- Tips for creating an in-house mediation program

Got Conflict? 5 styles for responding to conflict

- Cost of conflict in the workplace
- Understanding your personal style: accommodating, competing, compromising, avoiding and collaborating
- Identify which style is appropriate for a given situation

You have a choice: Mediate – Don't Litigate

- Understand differences between mediation, arbitration and litigation
- Principles of mediation: neutral, confidential, voluntary
- Benefits of using mediation to improve communication and productivity

Beyond Reason: Understanding Emotions in Negotiation

- Identify 5 core concerns: appreciation, affiliation, autonomy, status, role
- Application of core concerns to a negotiation
- Negotiation tips

Dr. Richard Deems

Richard S Deems, PhD, has been quoted in Wall Street Journal, New York Times, Atlanta Journal-Constitution, CNBC News, CareerBuilder, The Ladders, Monster com and even The Sporting News. He is the author of 12 books on key management issues, and co-author with his daughter Terri A Deems, PhD, of the 5-Star books Leading In Tough Times and Make Job Loss Work For You.

Deems is founding president of WorkLife Design, with offices in Arizona, Iowa, and Illinois. WorkLife Design works in all segments of the economy, including finance, insurance, manufacturing, retail, higher education, non-profits, and healthcare. Their client's revenues range from $5M to $40B.

A popular speaker, Deems has presented more than 2,000 keynotes, executive seminars, and workshops from coast to coast. He's presented at ASTD Regional, International, and Leadership Conferences, and consistently receives high evaluations. One participant reported, "Didn't get my afternoon nap," and another said, "We got more than our money's worth."

Hot Topics:

- **Taking Care of Your Own Career**

- **How to Turn Job Hunting into Job Getting**

- **High Performance – Doing What Comes Naturally**

- **Why Everyone Doesn't React to Change the Same Way**

- **Crush the Biggest Mistake Executives Make**

- **Putting the Right Person in the Right Seat In the…**

- **Developing Support for Change When the Stakeholders Didn't Create It**

Jack Dermody

Jack Dermody (UCLA, MA) has worked to advance human communication and personal relationships for thirty years through language and psychology. He is a corporate trainer, group facilitator, and consultant.

Beyond Four Windows temperament creations, he lights fires under teams and demonstrates effective communication, actual conflict management, and personal development. His clients include corporations and government organizations on five continents.

Interesting career notes.

- Created the prized Four Windows Personality Survey
- Writes the weekly newsletter "Personality Matters"
- Is in high-demand as a corporate facilitator
- Founded the Speakers Resource Organization (SRO)
- Was Curriculum and Training Coordinator for the City of Phoenix;
- Wrote 13 books on language learning
- Headed marketing and sales for international publisher
- Began his career in the Peace Corps in West Africa

Hot Topics:

SATISFY 4 TYPES OF PROSPECTS TO CLOSE MOST SALES: How Personality-Driven Companies Rule the Marketplace

- The Types: The Careful, The Impulsive, The Idealistic, The Expert
- The "personality" of your product matters
- Your style of communication counts more than you may know
- Examples abound of major-league, personality-driven companies

HIRE YOUR WEAKNESSES AND WIN: Acknowledging a Need for Help Trumps Staying Stupid (...and Mediocre)

- Identfying and living with your deficits
- Delegating with skill and joy
- Leveraging your strengths
- Dominating the marketplace

SURE, BUILD YOUR TEAM, BUT MOVE THEM TO <u>ACT</u>: Teams Need a Leader with Persuasive Skills

- Calling a group of people a team does not make them a team
- Who are your leaders? What are their significant strengths and costly weaknesses?
- Persuasion is a skill that everybody can learn
- By demanding persistent action, you never settle for second-rate

MANAGE CONFLICT BY CREATING A CULTURE OF PERSONALITIES: It's Hard to Get Mad When You Quickly Assess Where People Are Really Coming From

- Choosing temperament assessment tools that balance the playing field for Harvard graduates and high school dropouts
- Understanding self and (almost) all others
- Changing communication in the whole organization in days or weeks
- Making positive, authentic changes and keeping them on the front burner forever

IS YOUR WELLNESS PROGRAM SAVING YOU HEALTH INSURANCE MONEY? The Only Fitness Program That Works Is the One That Will Cater to Individual Styles

- Healthcare insurance companies want to reward low-risk fitness
- Getting fit and staying fit is difficult and complex at every levels
- Competent education and training cost far less than the premiums you are paying now
- Real fitness happens when people know their real selves and what is really possible

Valerie Harper

 Valerie Harper is creator/owner of True Wealth Consulting. She offers private consultations, group lectures and has authored 24 books on navigating the inner self. She writes screenplays and specializes in assisting people put together their personal stories so they can better understand their psychology so they can live with better love, harmony, vibrant health and prosperity.

"As a true wealth consultant I assist people in removing their inner obstacles to getting what they want. There are many different approaches to wellness that no longer takes 20 years of therapy. My work is based on a new approach to psychological design. What people used to cope with now stops them from living with authentic fulfillment and success. Each presentation is designed to cultivate a deeper sense of inner awareness to help you thrive in a specific way." –Valerie Harper

Main Topics for Presentations Include:

- Calculating Your Wealth Formula

- The Abundance of Self

- The Tao of Alternative Healing

- Emotional Traumas that Lead to Poverty

- The Love Veteran's Relationship Course on Unrequited Love

Mary Henry

Mary Henry, President and Founder of HR on Demand, a business consulting firm that specializes in adding bottom line value to organizations through business development and sound human resource practices. Her company was founded in 2009, and serves business' of all sizes throughout the metro Phoenix area.

Prior to founding her own company, Mary spent 10+ years at a Fortune 50 company, serving in roles such as training and development, recruiting, employee relations, people development and various other projects and disciplines throughout the organization.

She has both small business and the large corporate experience. She holds the SPHR, Senior Professional in Human Resource designation from the Society of Human Resource Management.

Hot Topics:

How to get the most from your team and retain top talent.

Objectives of the program:

- Define engagement and the business case for doing so.
- How to provide feedback
- Performance management templates and tools

Unemployment: How to manage the process and claims.

Objectives of the program

- Program Guidelines
- Tax and Work Programs
- Best practices to avoid turnover

NLRB and unfair labor practices

- Identify the agencies governing employee rights.
- Determine the scope of their jurisdiction in employee relations issues
- Employee rights under these statutes
- Employer rights under these statutes
- Tools and tips for good employee relations

Minimizing turnover through effective sourcing, interviewing, assessing, and hiring.

- Understand how candidates search for jobs
- The impact of competency based interview questions
- When and how to administer pre-employment assessments

Allan Himmelstein

With a 30+ year track record of driving multimillion dollar revenue growth Allan Himmelstein is a trusted advisor and decisive sales leader. His extensive business management experience includes the startup of an international company, which grew to $40,000,000 in nine years, and serving as VP of Sales and Marketing for a $50,000,000 ConAgra company. Allan's expertise includes:

- Tactical sales and Marketing Planning
- Hiring the best sales and sales management for your particular need
- Best practices for managing, measuring, and motivating a sales force
- Sales coaching and mentoring.

Hot Topics:

Getting In the Door Without Cold Calling

We are all Accidental Sales People, and every business needs to sell. Learn proven sales strategies for getting in the door even if you have never sold before and without cold calling.

Handling the Appointment and Getting the Sale

The shortest Sales course in the world is "Ask Questions and Listen". However there is a process and a method to asking the right questions that eventually lead to a sale. This workshop will increase your opportunities to open new business.

10 Biggest Mistakes of Sales Managers

How many times have you heard, "My Salespeople Can't Sell?" Have we hired correctly? Have we given them the right tools? Have we made them into clerks or customer sales representatives? These answers and more will be covered, discussed, with some suggested solutions.

Karen Laughlin

 Karen Laughlin, SPHR, started Thomas Resources to develop leaders and provide opportunities for diverse professionals. Karen is a human capital specialist with over a decade of talent acquisition strategy, delivery and retention program experience with Fortune 100 companies.

Program management, executive coaching on talent strategies and project management of national recruiting events are additional accomplishments during her career. Karen naturally excels at building and maintaining valuable relationships with clients by listening to needs, identifying common ground and providing targeted solutions. Raised in a military family and living in multi-cultural environments developed Karen's passion for inclusion and the work of diversity.

Hot Topics:

American Values in the Workplace

During this session we will reminisce about the good old days in our organizations then consider our responsibility to maintain the American culture of leadership, innovation and excellence of being #1!

Specifically we'll review the following values and their impact on business performance and effective people resource management:

- Accountability
- Responsibility
- Engagement
- Performance excellence

Customer focused orientation (internal and external)

Career Management: Different outcomes for men and women

Career advancement strategies for women based on the recent Catalyst report "The Myth of the Ideal Worker: Does Doing all the Right Things Really Get Women Ahead?"

- Use information from this report to manage the career advancement of ourselves or of individuals who report to us
- Review factors that impact gender pay disparities
- Career Management impact on promotions, pay increases & job satisfaction

Social Media: Your personal Career Assistant

Social Media is free, always open and offers new resources daily. Learn how to launch then navigate these resources to land your next great job by connecting with people in the real world!

- Review current job search & unemployment trends
- Learn how and why to become a social media voyeur on... LinkedIn - Google+ - Twitter - Pinterest - Facebook
- Actions that lead to influential connections and securing interviews
- Extra Credit – Use social media to establish/brand yourself as a subject matter expert in your respective field

Motivation: The Key to making better people decisions

Regardless if we're hiring or identifying strategic partners to meet client expectations, being aware of individuals' motivations & values will enable you to make better choices, minimize risk, reduce problems & waste of valuable resources.

- Discover the components to identify, confirm and analyze potential partner's motivation thru questions, active listening & analysis
- Create a process map to improve the decisions made about staff or partners

Dr. Kristine Quade

 Dr Kristine Quade focuses on accomplishing what others say is impossible. Keenly aware of the accelerating dynamics of uncontrollable change, Kristine has developed creative solutions for identifying the difference that makes a difference and guiding actions that are both flexible and realistic.

Her area of expertise includes leadership, global strategic thinking, creativity and innovation, team effectiveness and influencing the dynamics of discontinuous change.

Key Accomplishments:

- Worked with over 150 client systems in over 20 countries
- Author of 5 books and numerous articles on change
- Attorney and Doctorate in Organizational Change
- Founder of the Dynamical Leadership Academy
- Frequent keynote presenter at management conferences

Areas of Expertise:

Leadership, Organizational and Personal Effectiveness, Dynamics of Change

Hot Topics:

Simple Rules: The Leaders Guide to Navigating Unpredictable Change

- What creates the bond that holds members of a unit in coordinated action?
- What rallies individuals around a common cause?
- What guides individuals to make good decisions during a crisis?

The answer is in the concept of simple rules that find a balance between data and intuition, planning and acting, safety and risk, autonomy and control, and change and stability.

What the Bleep Do We Know About Change?

- Mechanistic approaches to change are no longer working.
- Complexity of change is magnifying what is broken.
- Unpredictability creates tension to over-correct

Want to understand the complex dynamics of change in a meaningful way? Want to become more resilient when needing to adapt? Want to identify the patterns of the emerging unknown?

Early Warning Systems: Seeing and Influencing Patterns During Challenging Times

Patterns that have influenced leadership decisions in the past have included competition, revenue, employee opinion and performance and environmental trends. There are more patterns at play that most don't see because they have been trained to look for what is traditional.

This session will:

- Create an awareness of the shadow patterns that influence environmental, organizational and individual behavior.
- Identify a different way of thinking about patterns.
- Create an understanding of the conditions that shape the speed, path and outcome of a pattern

Dynamical Leadership: Accomplishing What Others Say is Impossible

Dynamical change results from multiple forces acting in unpredictable ways, generating surprising outcomes. The Leadership Landscape Diagram

- Creates an understanding of the forces at play
- Outlines the key factors leaders need to be paying attention to
- Identifies power points that will influence change
- Defines key leadership competencies for leading during times of rapid change

Ray Silverstein

Ray Silverstein is a small business expert, advocate, and author known for his humorous, insightful, business parables and presentations.

Ray has spent decades collecting and studying real-life stories of entrepreneurial success and failure. He has shared many of them in his books, "The Best Secrets of Great Small Business" and "The Small Business Survival Guide." He is an online columnist for the *Phoenix Business Journal* and has contributed numerous articles to *Entrepreneur.com*.

Ray knows a thing or two about success. He has owned, grown, and sold several businesses, including a hand tool manufacturing company and automotive parts company that he grew into multi-million dollar enterprises before divesting them in the 1980s.

Today, Ray talks to hundreds of business professionals each month, discussing every aspect of running and growing a business, from sales and marketing to finance and leadership. One of his favorite expressions is the ancient proverb, *All of Us Are Smarter than One of Us.*

Ray works out of Phoenix and Chicago.

Hot Topics:

What's in the Secret Sauce? – 7 surprise ingredients for success.

The cookie-cutter approach to success doesn't work for every business. In this entrepreneurial seminar, attendees will learn the seven surprise ingredients for creating their own successful "secret sauce," some which include:

- Entrepreneurial DNA
- The Crown Jewels
- The Art of Differentiation

Ready, Set, Grow – Best practices for building successful sales

If sales aren't growing, the company can't either. In this roll-up-your-sleeves workshop, we'll review the best practices for building a successful sales organization. Attendees will learn how to:

- Craft an effective USP (Unique Sales Proposition)
- Define your Sales Funnel to maximize success
- Hire the right kind of salesperson for your organization.
- Taking referrals to a whole new level!

Send Your Sales Skyrocketing – Steps for firing up your sales force, elevating your brand, and landing the customers you want most.

So many companies would like to hit the 'reset' button on sales performance. Invite them to this workshop instead! We'll learn how to give sales operations a step-by-step tune-up that will boost results into overdrive. Topic Areas include…

- Tips for firing up a sales force (no, it isn't about commission!)
- How to elevate your brand
- Smoothing out, and ramping up, your sales process
- Best ways to land the customers you want most

Understanding the Corporate Life Cycle – As companies develop, they face different requirements and challenges. Give your business what it needs to stay healthy at every stage.

As companies develop, they face different requirements and challenges. Whether just starting up or coasting along, companies at every stage will learn how to give their business what it needs now, and it what it will need in the future. We'll discuss:

- Phases of the corporate life cycle (where are you?)
- The benefits and pitfalls of every stage
- Questions you should be asking yourself
- How to stay ahead of the curve

Dr. Terri Trent

Terri Trent is a knowledgeable business focused organizational consultant, executive coach, and facilitator, who specializes in providing innovative business solutions for both organizations and individuals. She has more than twenty years of diverse experience in organizational change, executive coaching, performance management, leadership development, group facilitation, curriculum design, and business communications.

Terri's current focus and specific areas of expertise include executive coaching, assessment of organizational effectiveness, curriculum design using adult learning theory, group facilitation, leadership development, change management, diversity training, team building, competency development, conflict resolution, and multiple assessments, including the StrengthsFinder and Myers-Briggs Type Inventory.

In addition to her current consulting work, Terri is an online graduate instructor in organizational development and human resources management at both DeVry University and the University of Phoenix.

Hot Topics:

Leadership

- Creating an Engaging Workplace: A Guide for Leaders & Managers
- Using Psychological Type and Temperament to Develop and Strengthen Teams

Diversity

- Multiple Generations at Work
- Respecting and Valuing Diversity
- Unlock Your Career Potential by Developing Talents and Strengths

Personal Effectiveness

- The Bounce Back: Developing Resiliency Through the White Waters of Change
- Making Career Connections: Strategies for Managing Your Career in a Changing World of Work

Communication

- Negotiation Strategies that Create a Win-Win Outcome
- Persuasion Strategies for Maximum Impact
- Creative Facilitation Techniques for Trainers and Facilitators
- Emotional Intelligence at Work: Why it is as Important as IQ for Achieving Workplace Success

Elena Zee

 In her eighteen year career, Elena Zee has done business in more than twenty countries, responsible for Risk Management, Portfolio Management, Customer Service and Information Management.

Elena has a Master's Degree in Economics from Columbia University as a President Fellow and Double Bachelor's degrees in Economics and Math from Wellesley College. She was born and raised in Shanghai, China and often coaches individuals and businesses on working with China and understanding people from the Chinese culture.

Elena is on the Board of Arizona Council on Economic Education, Chinese Chamber of Commerce of Arizona, Arizona Humanities Council and Co-President of Phi Beta Kappa Phoenix Association.

Hot Topics:

Win business and work effectively with the Chinese culture

- Chinese history
- Chinese culture vs. American culture
- How to win the Chinese business

Current Affairs and China – open forum discussion

- International Trade
- Human Rights
- Environment and Politics

Chinese Economy

- Centrally planned system vs. free market system
- Labor market
- Housing

Chinese calligraphy and cuisine

- History of the calligraphy and practice
- Introduction to different cuisines
- Cuisine field trip

SPEAKERS RESOURCE ORGANIZATION

SPEAKERS RESOURCE ORGANIZATION

Speakers Resource Organization is a dedicated group of seasoned professionals with a variety of industry backgrounds and expertise who provide thought-provoking presentations and great takeaways. We are proud of the high level of experienced educators and facilitators that we have attracted. We specialize in serving the needs of organizations, business advisory groups, corporations and non-profit groups.

Our goals are to maintain integrity with quality delivery that exceeds client expectations and to engage in generative learning. We are committed to helping create great events through information, sharing and teaching. Looking for a specific topic or time frame? We can assist with either, made to order.

If you or someone you know is interested in becoming a member and has the skills and experience to deliver top-notch presentations, please contact us. Joining SRO will put you in contact not only with organizations, but with professionals who can help you develop your skills as a professional speaker, including a variety of technical services to help your web presence.

We provide 20-, 40- and 60-minute presentations to meet the variety of scheduling needs for your company, group or organization. If you would like to book a speaker, please visit our website and use our **Contact Page**.

On the following pages you will find our speakers' bios, descriptions and a list of hot topics. If you don't see exactly what you are looking for, no doubt our presenters can craft a presentation specifically to your needs. To view individual websites and/or blogs you can visit our **Presenters** page on the website. Visit our website:
www.SpeakersResourceOrganization.com

www.ingramcontent.com/pod-product-compliance
Lightning Source LLC
Chambersburg PA
CBHW071814170526
45167CB00003B/1305